TO

FROM

Trust in the LORD with all your heart
    and lean not on your own understanding;
in all your ways acknowledge him,
    and he will make your paths straight.

Proverbs 3:5–6

For the Graduate
Copyright 2000 by ZondervanPublishingHouse

ISBN 0-310-97808-4

Requests for information should be addressed to:
    Inspirio, the Gift Group of Zondervan
    Grand Rapids, Michigan 49530

Senior editor: Gwen Ellis
Compiler: Robin Schmitt
Design: Mark Veldheer
Cover photograph ©Superstock Inc./Scott Barrow
Interior photography by Comstock, Digital Stock, Eyewire Images, Photodisc, and Mark Veldheer

Printed in China
03 / ❖ HK / 8 7 6

FOR THE GRADUATE

God's Guidance for the Road Ahead

inspirio

The gift group of Zondervan

Table of Contents

ACCOUNTABILITY

Pursue righteousness, faith, love and peace, along with those who call on the Lord out of a pure heart.

2 TIMOTHY 2:22

I sometimes attended AA as an act of solidarity with a recovering alcoholic friend. The first time I accompanied him I was overwhelmed by what I found, for in many ways it resembled the New Testament church. A well-known television broadcaster and several prominent millionaires mixed freely with unemployed dropouts and kids who wore Band-Aids to hide the needle marks on their arms. The "sharing time" was like a textbook small group, marked by compassionate listening, warm responses, and many hugs.

Introductions went like this: "Hi, I'm Tom, and I'm an alcoholic and a drug addict." Instantly everyone shouted out in unison, like a Greek chorus, "Hi, Tom!" Each person attending gave a personal progress report on his or her battle with addiction.

Over time I saw that AA runs on two principles: radical honesty and radical dependence. These are the very same principles expressed in the Lord's Prayer, Jesus' capsule summary of living "one day at a time," and in fact many AA groups recite the Lord's Prayer together at each meeting.

For a "cure," the AA program demands of its members radical dependence on a Higher Power and on fellow strugglers. Most people in the groups I've attended substitute "God" for "Higher Power." They openly ask God for forgiveness and strength, and ask their friends around them for support. They come to AA because they believe that there grace flows "on tap."

PHILIP YANCEY

After Mike [a buddy from the Houston Oilers] had been out of football for a while, I asked him what he missed most about pro ball. I was surprised by his answer. He said it was when they got in the huddle on the field. I asked him why. He replied that in the huddle you felt safe. It was a place where you could come and get encouragement, direction, support, and correction. It was also a place where you could regroup for the next phase of the battle and know that you had ten other guys with you to help you win....

Like Mike, every man needs the huddle. He needs a safe place where he can go and get what he needs to enter into the next phase of life's conflict. If a man's going to survive—no, win—the battles of his life, he must have a huddle of good men around him to cheer him on and bandage his wounds in the midst of the fight. He needs to know that he has men around him who will celebrate with him in the good times and do whatever it takes to bring help and healing in the bad times.

RODNEY L. COOPER

Encourage one another and build each other up.

1 Thessalonians 5:11

No temptation has seized you except what is common to man. And God is faithful; he will not let you be tempted beyond what you can bear. But when you are tempted, he will also provide a way out so that you can stand up under it.

1 Corinthians 10:13

Jesus said, "Where two or three come together in my name, there am I with them."

Matthew 18:20

Though one may be overpowered,
    two can defend themselves.
A cord of three strands is not quickly
    broken.

Ecclesiastes 4:12

As iron sharpens iron,
    so one man sharpens another.

Proverbs 27:17

He who walks with the wise grows wise.

Proverbs 13:20

Confess your sins to each other and pray for each other so that you may be healed.

James 5:16

Pray in the Spirit on all occasions with all kinds of prayers and requests. With this in mind, be alert and always keep on praying for all the saints.

Ephesians 6:18

The pleasantness of one's friend
    springs from his earnest counsel.

Proverbs 27:9

Carry each other's burdens, and in this way you will fulfill the law of Christ.

Galatians 6:2

Two are better than one,
    because they have a good return
        for their work:
If one falls down,
    his friend can help him up.

Ecclesiastes 4:9–10

ACHIEVEMENT

Godliness with contentment is great gain. For we brought nothing into the world, and we can take nothing out of it.

1 TIMOTHY 6:6–7

How do you measure success? Is it a moving target, an elusive something that you never know if you have?…

Success isn't in the money that you make, the job that you have, the way that you look, the car that you drive, the beauty of the person to whom you're married, the awards that you've achieved. Because then success does become a moving target.

Instead success must be found in something consistent and attainable, something that can sustain satisfaction. Jesus said, "I have come that they may have life, and have it to the full" (John 10:10). Defining success must begin first and foremost on a spiritual level. A relationship with Jesus Christ gives us an unmovable source of acceptance, love, and strength that enables us to face changes, failures, and the pressures of society. Success is found in a personal relationship with Jesus Christ. Otherwise success is a moving target. Standards change and feelings fade. But Christ is consistent, unchanging, solid.

DENNY RYDBERG

Grace is God's kindness and graciousness toward humanity without regard to the worth or merit of those who receive it and in spite of the fact that they don't deserve it. God's grace toward the believer means that we cannot do anything to make God love us any less or any more. Think on that!

What this does (to type-A personalities like me, as well as to every other human disposition) is dismantle the tiresome treadmill of performance. I don't have to be successful to be loved. I don't have to fulfill certain obligations to be loved. I am loved by the God of all grace because there is nothing I can do to earn or merit his love.

Are you working hard to gain God's favor? You have it. Is there always something more you think you have to do in order to be accepted? God has done all you need through the cross of Christ to make you acceptable…. Christ's performance on the cross has been credited to your account so you can be free to live life "to the full" (John 10:10).

CHARLES STANLEY

LORD, *you have assigned me my portion and my cup;*
you have made my lot secure.
The boundary lines have fallen for me in pleasant places;
surely I have a delightful inheritance.
You have made known to me the path of life;
you will fill me with joy in your presence,
with eternal pleasures at your right hand.

PSALM 16:5–6, 11

Jesus said, "Where your treasure is, there your heart will be also."

Matthew 6:21

Each one should be careful how he builds. For no one can lay any foundation other than the one already laid, which is Jesus Christ. If any man builds on this foundation using gold, silver, costly stones, wood, hay or straw, his work will be shown for what it is, because the Day will bring it to light. It will be revealed with fire, and the fire will test the quality of each man's work. If what he has built survives, he will receive his reward.

1 Corinthians 3:10–14

The word of the LORD came to Abram in a vision: "Do not be afraid, Abram. I am your shield, your very great reward."

Genesis 15:1

Jesus said, "Behold, I am coming soon! My reward is with me, and I will give to everyone according to what he has done."

Revelation 22:12

Jesus said, "After a long time the master of those servants returned and settled accounts with them. The man who had received the five talents brought the other five. 'Master,' he said, 'you entrusted me with five talents. See, I have gained five more.' His master replied, 'Well done, good and faithful servant! You have been faithful with a few things; I will put you in charge of many things. Come and share your master's happiness!'"

Matthew 25:19–21

One thing I ask of the LORD,
    this is what I seek:
that I may dwell in the house of the
    LORD
    all the days of my life,
to gaze upon the beauty of the LORD
    and to seek him in his temple.

Psalm 27:4

Jesus said, "Everyone who hears these words of mine and puts them into practice is like a wise man who built his house on the rock. The rain came down, the streams rose, and the winds blew and beat against that house; yet it did not fall, because it had its foundation on the rock."

Matthew 7:24–25

Jesus said, "Remain in me, and I will remain in you. No branch can bear fruit by itself; it must remain in the vine. Neither can you bear fruit unless you remain in me. I am the vine; you are the branches. If a man remains in me and I in him, he will bear much fruit; apart from me you can do nothing.... I chose you and appointed you to go and bear fruit— fruit that will last."

John 15:4–5, 16

ATTITUDE

Your attitude should be the same as that of Christ Jesus:
Who, being in very nature God,
did not consider equality with God something
to be grasped,
but made himself nothing,
taking the very nature of a servant,
being made in human likeness.
And being found in appearance as a man,
he humbled himself
and became obedient to death —
even death on a cross!
Therefore God exalted him to the highest place
and gave him the name that is above every name,
that at the name of Jesus every knee should bow,
in heaven and on earth and under the earth,
and every tongue confess that Jesus Christ is Lord,
to the glory of God the Father.

PHILIPPIANS 2:5–11

By faith Abraham, when called to go to a place he would later receive his inheritance, obeyed and went, even though he did not know where he was going.

HEBREWS 11:8

Continually revise your attitude towards God and see if it is a going out of everything, trusting in God entirely. It is this attitude that keeps you in perpetual wonder—you do not know what God is going to do next. Each morning you wake, it is to be a "going out," building in confidence on God. "Take no thought for your life, . . . nor yet for your body"—take no thought for the things for which you did take thought before you "went out."

Have you been asking God what He is going to do? He will never tell you. God does not tell you what He is going to do; He reveals to you who He is. Do you believe in a miracle-working God, and will you go out in surrender to Him until you are not surprised an atom at anything He does?

Suppose God is the God you know Him to be when you are nearest to Him—what an impertinence worry is! Let the attitude of the life be a continual "going out" in dependence upon God, and your life will have an ineffable charm about it which is a satisfaction to Jesus.

OSWALD CHAMBERS

Be still and know that I am God.

PSALM 46:10

It was 2:20 A.M. I suddenly awakened from a restful sleep, sensing God had something to say to me. In a matter of seconds, Psalm 46 came to mind. I turned on the light and began to read....

The tenth verse arrested my soul: "Be still and know that I am God." In the quiet of the night, I knew God was revealing something that I desperately needed to know. I prayed, asking God to open up the meaning of the verse so that I might receive his fullness, and then I returned to bed.

The next morning I met with a group of pastors. As we prayed together, I shared my experience with one. He opened his Bible and read Psalm 46:10 from another translation (NASB): "Cease striving and know that I am God."

As soon as I heard the words "cease striving," I knew what God was saying to me.... I breathed a sigh of spiritual relief as I saw the futility of my attempts to carry out God's commands with my resources and his amazing adequacy for every demand. I can "cease striving" to be holy and righteous, because "in Christ" I already am holy and righteous. I don't have to strain to gain God's approval, because he already loves me unconditionally.

Do you see how this removes the struggle? Do you understand how this can help you to relax and rest in the all-sufficiency of God's grace? Christ, who indwells you through the Holy Spirit, is your peace, strength, comfort, wisdom, hope, joy, and guide. You have all this because you have Christ.

CHARLES STANLEY

Blessed are the poor in spirit,

for theirs is the kingdom of heaven.

Blessed are those who mourn,

for they will be comforted.

Blessed are the meek,

for they will inherit the earth.

Blessed are those who hunger and thirst for righteousness,

for they will be filled.

Blessed are the merciful,

for they will be shown mercy.

Blessed are the pure in heart,

for they will see God.

Matthew 5:3–8

What does the LORD require of you? To act justly and to love mercy and to walk humbly with your God.

Micah 6:8

Rejoice in the Lord always. I will say it again: Rejoice! Let your gentleness be evident to all. The Lord is near. Do not be anxious about anything, but in everything, by prayer and petition, with thanksgiving, present your requests to God. And the peace of God, which transcends all understanding, will guard your hearts and your minds in Christ Jesus. Finally, brothers, whatever is true, whatever is noble, whatever is right, whatever is pure, whatever is lovely, whatever is admirable— if anything is excellent or praiseworthy—think about such things.

Philippians 4:4–8

Whoever humbles himself will be exalted.

Matthew 23:12

Let the peace of Christ rule in your hearts, since as members of one body you were called to peace. And be thankful. Let the word of Christ dwell in you richly as you teach and admonish one another with all wisdom, and as you sing psalms, hymns and spiritual songs with gratitude in your hearts to God. And whatever you do, whether in word or deed, do it all in the name of the Lord Jesus, giving thanks to God the Father through him.

Colossians 3:15–17

Do not conform any longer to the pattern of this world, but be transformed by the renewing of your mind. Then you will be able to test and approve what God's will is — his good, pleasing and perfect will.

Romans 12:2

CHANGE

"I know the plans I have for you," declares the LORD, "plans to prosper you and not to harm you, plans to give you hope and a future."

JEREMIAH 29:11

When I was a child, I learned a song that went something like this: "Make new friends but keep the old; one is silver, the other gold."

I like the idea expressed in that song, but frankly, keeping old friends is not always possible, for several reasons. One is the sheer weight of all those friendships on life. If you keep adding new friendships and never let some of the old ones go, you'll spend all your time just trying to stay in contact and be a good friend "to everyone." The other reason is that life simply doesn't allow you to keep all old friends. Old friends move, change interests, and grow apart for legitimate reasons.

So I'd like to edit the childhood song, "Make a few new friends but keep a few old; one is silver, the other gold."

DENNY RYDBERG

Often we want to be able to see into the future. We say, "How will next year be for me? Where will I be five or ten years from now?" There are no answers to these questions. Mostly we have just enough light to see the next step: what we have to do in the coming hour or the following day. The art of living is to enjoy what we can see and not complain about what remains in the dark. When we are able to take the next step with the trust that we will have enough light for the step that follows, we can walk through life with joy and be surprised at how far we go. Let's rejoice in the little light we carry and not ask for the great beam that would take all shadows away.

HENRI J. M. NOUWEN

In all things God works for the good of those who love him, who have been called according to his purpose. For those God foreknew he also predestined to be conformed to the likeness of his Son, that he might be the firstborn among many brothers. And those he predestined, he also called; those he called, he also justified; those he justified, he also glorified. What, then, shall we say in response to this? If God is for us, who can be against us?

ROMANS 8:28–31

If anyone is in Christ, he is a new creation; the old
has gone, the new has come!

2 Corinthians 5:17

Where can I go from your Spirit?
    Where can I flee from your presence?
If I go up to the heavens, you are there;
    if I make my bed in the depths, you are there.
If I rise on the wings of the dawn,
    if I settle on the far side of the sea,
even there your hand will guide me,
    your right hand will hold me fast.

Psalm 139:7–10

Every good and perfect gift is from above, coming down from the Father of the heavenly lights, who does not change like shifting shadows.

James 1:17

I pray that you, being rooted and established in love, may have power, together with all the saints, to grasp how wide and long and high and deep is the love of Christ.

Ephesians 3:17–18

You were taught, with regard to your former way of life, to put off your old self, which is being corrupted by its deceitful desires; to be made new in the attitude of your minds; and to put on the new self, created to be like God in true righteousness and holiness.

Ephesians 4:22–24

When I was a child, I talked like a child, I thought like a child, I reasoned like a child. When I became a man, I put childish ways behind me.

1 Corinthians 13:11

"Though the mountains be shaken
 and the hills be removed,
yet my unfailing love for you will
  not be shaken
 nor my covenant of peace be
  removed,"
 says the LORD, who has compassion on you.

Isaiah 54:10

Neither death nor life, neither angels nor demons, neither the present nor the future, nor any powers, neither height nor depth, nor anything else in all creation, will be able to separate us from the love of God that is in Christ Jesus our Lord.

Romans 8:38–39

Listen, I tell you a mystery: We will not all sleep, but we will all be changed — in a flash, in the twinkling of an eye, at the last trumpet.

1 Corinthians 15:51–52

CHARACTER

Let love and faithfulness never leave you;
bind them around your neck,
write them on the tablet of your heart.
Then you will win favor and a good name
in the sight of God and man.

Trust in the LORD with all your heart
and lean not on your own understanding;
in all your ways acknowledge him,
and he will make your paths straight.

PROVERBS 3:3–6

Live a life worthy of the calling you have received. Be completely humble and gentle; be patient, bearing with one another in love.

EPHESIANS 4:1–2

Humility involves a Copernican revolution of the soul, the realization that the universe does not revolve around us. Humility always brings a kind of relief.

A friend named Gwen Bird was teaching a Sunday school class and decided to have the children "reenact" the Creation. This required children to portray animals and plant life. One six-year-old, whom we will call Jonathan, was assigned to stand on a ladder and shine a flashlight on the whole proceedings. He was supposed to represent God. Just about the time the creeping things were starting to creep over to where the swimming things were supposed to swim, Gwen felt a tug on her skirt. It was "God." He wanted out. "I'm just feeling too crazy to be God today," said Jonathan. "Could you get somebody else?"

Humility, if ever we could grow into it, would not be a burden. It would be an immense gift. Humility is the freedom to stop trying to be what we're not, or pretending to be what we're not, and accepting our "appropriate smallness." In Luther's words, humility is the decision to "let God be God."

JOHN ORTBERG

Generosity is the hallmark of genuine Christianity. "A generous man will prosper; he who refreshes others will himself be refreshed" (Proverbs 11:25). Giving is the channel through which the love of God flows.

A generous person is happy. Others are drawn to a generous person, not for a handout, but because of the inviting spiritual atmosphere that surrounds him. A generous person is sensitive to the needs of others and gives genuinely, not for the purpose of manipulation. He receives joy in seeing others benefit from his benevolence. He views needs as an opportunity, not a threat. He wants to see how much he can give, not how little. He trusts God for his own needs.

Generosity opens the heart of both giver and recipient to the lavish love of Christ. Both can become spiritually wealthy and prosperous, enjoying the riches of the Christ-centered life. If you are reluctant to give, stingy with your resources, and isolated from the needs of others, you're missing out on fantastic blessings from your generous heavenly Father. "Give and it will be given to you," Jesus promised (Luke 6:38). Such is the power of generosity. It is the right choice to make. Give something today and watch God work.

CHARLES STANLEY

Be imitators of God, therefore, as dearly loved children and live a life of love, just as Christ loved us and gave himself up for us as a fragrant offering and sacrifice to God.

Ephesians 5:1–2

May God himself, the God of peace, sanctify you through and through. May your whole spirit, soul and body be kept blameless at the coming of our Lord Jesus Christ. The one who calls you is faithful and he will do it.

1 Thessalonians 5:23–24

Just as he who called you is holy, so be holy in all you do; for it is written: "Be holy, because I am holy."

1 Peter 1:15–16

You are light in the Lord. Live as children of light (for the fruit of the light consists in all goodness, righteousness and truth) and find out what pleases the Lord.

Ephesians 5:8–10

Since we belong to the day, let us be self-controlled, putting on faith and love as a breastplate, and the hope of salvation as a helmet.

1 Thessalonians 5:8

The fruit of the Spirit is love, joy, peace, patience, kindness, goodness, faithfulness, gentleness and self-control. Against these there is no law.

Galatians 5:22–23

The wisdom that comes from heaven is first of all pure; then peace-loving, considerate, submissive, full of mercy and good fruit, impartial and sincere.

James 3:17

Who is wise and understanding among you? Let him show it by his good life, by deeds done in the humility that comes from wisdom.

James 3:13

Humility and the fear of the LORD
bring wealth and honor and life.

Proverbs 22:4

It is God who works in you to will and to act according to his good purpose.

Philippians 2:13

A good name is more desirable than
great riches;
to be esteemed is better than silver
or gold.

Proverbs 22:1

COMMUNICATION

Speak to one another with psalms, hymns and spiritual songs. Sing and make music in your heart to the Lord, always giving thanks to God the Father for everything, in the name of our Lord Jesus Christ.

EPHESIANS 5:19–20

The words are still hung and framed neatly and permanently. Not on my wall, but in my mind. They were spoken when I was only six years old. One memorable day, as I was leaving my school room, I overheard my teacher comment to another, "I like Charles." It was the first time a person other than my mom had ever said she liked me. I was elated. Her three simple words were high-octane emotional fuel that boosted my confidence and even changed the way I viewed myself.

Have you ever thought how influential the words you speak are? Do you know what kind of impact your speech can have on a person who desperately needs to hear an encouraging word? Solomon wrote, "Pleasant words are a honeycomb, sweet to the soul and healing to the bones" (Proverbs 16:24). What a wonderful way to describe our conversation. It can be medicine to a weary soul, healing to a bruised spirit. Kind words, spoken in due season, are God's bridges of love.

CHARLES STANLEY

My youngest child, Daniel, is eight years old.... He loves to talk. And when he talks he expects me to listen attentively, which I often forget. I'll be reading the paper or watching TV while he talks away about some subject. If he surmises that I'm half listening or not listening at all, he will walk over to me, wave his hand in front of my eyes, and say, "Dad, are you in there?"

Edward G. Dobson

To listen is very hard, because it asks of us so much interior stability that we no longer need to prove ourselves by speeches, arguments, statements, or declarations. True listeners no longer have an inner need to make their presence known. They are free to receive, to welcome, to accept.

Listening is much more than allowing another to talk while waiting for a chance to respond. Listening is paying full attention to others and welcoming them into our very beings. The beauty of listening is that those who are listened to start feeling accepted, start taking their words more seriously and discovering their true selves. Listening is a form of spiritual hospitality.

Henri J. M. Nouwen

Let us hold unswervingly to the hope we profess, for he who promised is faithful. And let us consider how we may spur one another on toward love and good deeds. Let us not give up meeting together, as some are in the habit of doing, but let us encourage one another—and all the more as you see the Day approaching.

HEBREWS 10:23–25

A word aptly spoken

is like apples of gold in settings of silver.

Proverbs 25:11

When we put bits into the mouths of horses to make them obey us, we can turn the whole animal. Or take ships as an example. Although they are so large and are driven by strong winds, they are steered by a very small rudder wherever the pilot wants to go. Likewise the tongue is a small part of the body, but it makes great boasts.

James 3:3–5

Always be prepared to give an answer to everyone who asks you to give the reason for the hope that you have. But do this with gentleness and respect.

1 Peter 3:15

Everyone should be quick to listen, slow to speak.

James 1:19

Jesus said, "If your brother sins against you, go and show him his fault, just between the two of you. If he listens to you, you have won your brother over."

Matthew 18:15

Moses said to the LORD, "O Lord, I have never been eloquent, neither in the past nor since you have spoken to your servant. I am slow of speech and tongue." The LORD said to him, "Who gave man his mouth? Who makes him deaf or mute? Who gives him sight or makes him blind? Is it not I, the LORD? Now go; I will help you speak and will teach you what to say."

Exodus 4:10–12

Let the word of Christ dwell in you richly as you teach and admonish one another with all wisdom, and as you sing psalms, hymns and spiritual songs with gratitude in your hearts to God. And whatever you do, whether in word or deed, do it all in the name of the Lord Jesus, giving thanks to God the Father through him.

Colossians 3:16–17

A gentle answer turns away wrath.

Proverbs 15:1

How beautiful on the mountains
    are the feet of those who bring
        good news,
who proclaim peace,
    who bring good tidings,
    who proclaim salvation,
who say to Zion,
    "Your God reigns!"

Isaiah 52:7

Before a word is on my tongue
    you know it completely, O LORD.

Psalm 139:4

COMPASSION

As God's chosen people, holy and dearly loved, clothe your-
selves with compassion, kindness, humility, gentleness and
patience. Bear with each other and forgive whatever griev-
ances you may have against one another. Forgive as the
Lord forgave you. And over all these virtues put on love,
which binds them all together in perfect unity.

COLOSSIANS 3:12–14

The homeless old man knocked at my door. Something inside me said to invite him in.

The winter had taken its toll on the old man. I offered him something to eat. Soup was all he could handle due to his chronic stomach problems. While he ate, we chatted about life. I was a struggling college student. He was down on his luck. As he prepared to leave, I couldn't help noticing his threadbare winter clothing. The new fleece-lined gloves Mom had given me for Christmas would serve him well. Besides, I had an older pair. Tears welled up in his eyes as he put on the gloves, and I got a big lump in my throat. I told him to come back anytime for another cup of soup, but I never saw him again.

The Bible says we sometimes entertain angels and aren't even aware of it (see Hebrews 13:2). Jesus said when we've fed and clothed the least of his people, we've done it for him (see Matthew 25:40). I don't know if that old man was an angel or not, but it sure gave me deep pleasure to share my food and clothes with him.

VIC BLACK

The LORD is compassionate and gracious,
*   slow to anger, abounding in love....*
For as high as the heavens are above the earth,
*   so great is his love for those who fear him;*
as far as the east is from the west,
*   so far has he removed our transgressions from us.*
As a father has compassion on his children,
*   so the LORD has compassion on those who fear him.*

PSALM 103:8, 11–13

As an older, successful man, Handel did not forget his impoverished past. Rather, he chose to use his fortune as a means to help others less fortunate. The story behind his masterpiece Messiah reflects Handel's generosity.

The oratorio was commissioned by a Dublin charity wanting to premiere a piece for a benefit concert. That first performance, on April 13, 1742, raised four hundred pounds, enough to free 142 men from debtors' prison. The charitable event was just the first for what has become a true classic.

Handel himself conducted the Messiah more than thirty times, many of these concerts being benefits for a favorite charity, the Foundling Hospital. In his will, Handel stipulated that this work was to continue to be used for the hospital's benefit.

If your talent in any area brought you wealth if not fame, how would you respond? What would you do with that wealth? Would you simply increase your standard of living, buy a bigger house, upgrade your car and other "toys"? Or would you use it to meet the needs of others who have not known your good fortune?

PATRICK KAVANAUGH

Speak up for those who cannot speak for themselves,

for the rights of all who are destitute.

Speak up and judge fairly;

defend the rights of the poor and needy.

Proverbs 31:8–9

"Is not this the kind of fasting I have chosen:

to loose the chains of injustice

and untie the cords of the yoke,

to set the oppressed free

and break every yoke?

Is it not to share your food with the hungry

and to provide the poor wanderer with shelter—

when you see the naked, to clothe him,

and not to turn away from your own flesh and blood?

Then your light will break forth like the dawn,

and your healing will quickly appear;

then your righteousness will go before you,

and the glory of the LORD will be your rear guard."

Isaiah 58:6–8

The LORD longs to be gracious to you;
he rises to show you compassion.
For the LORD is a God of justice.
Blessed are all who wait for him!

Isaiah 30:18

Jesus went through all the towns and villages, teaching in their synagogues, preaching the good news of the kingdom and healing every disease and sickness. When he saw the crowds, he had compassion on them.

Matthew 9:35–36

Live in harmony with one another; be sympathetic, love as brothers, be compassionate and humble. Do not repay evil with evil or insult with insult, but with blessing, because to this you were called so that you may inherit a blessing.

1 Peter 3:8–9

Seek justice,
encourage the oppressed.
Defend the cause of the fatherless,
plead the case of the widow.

Isaiah 1:17

Be kind and compassionate to one another, forgiving each other, just as in Christ God forgave you.

Ephesians 4:32

Praise be to the God and Father of our Lord Jesus Christ, the Father of compassion and the God of all comfort, who comforts us in all our troubles, so that we can comfort those in any trouble with the comfort we ourselves have received from God.

2 Corinthians 1:3–4

The Spirit of the Sovereign LORD is
on me,
because the LORD has anointed me
to preach good news to the poor.
He has sent me to bind up the
brokenhearted,
to proclaim freedom for the captives
and release from darkness for the
prisoners.

Isaiah 61:1

DREAMS

*The LORD delights in those who fear him,
  who put their hope in his unfailing love.*

PSALM 147:11

God had planted a dream in my husband Bernard's heart—to buy an old church building and turn it into a hangout for high school and college students. But a local youth worker ominously predicted that the neighbors would take us to court or blackball us in our small town. Bernard doesn't care much for conflict, but he knew that God's hand was in this idea. So he gathered his courage, picked up the phone and dialed the number of the "hangout's" closest neighbor. Bernard asked, "What is your reaction to this idea and how do you think the other neighbors will take it?" The man's answer was a complete shock to us. "I have no problems with it at all," he said. "In fact, I will be your advocate with the other neighbors!" Bernard nearly passed out with relief!

Why such an unexpected, positive response? The Lord had gone before us to fight our battle. After this experience, our faith increased all the more. After overcoming a few more obstacles, we won the war. God gave us the church building and the courage to implement Bernard's dream!

JENA BORAH

Although he had his share of misfortunes, Mendelssohn, an optimistic man of strong Christian faith, was always quick to pull out of them and prevail. As a teenager, Mendelssohn set his heart on being a great musician—and he was.

When he "found" and promoted the long-ignored music of J. S. Bach, he expected everyone to share his enthusiasm. And they did. One of his desires was to create a great music school. He opened the doors of the renowned Leipzig Conservatory of Music in 1843, and it has since schooled many of Europe's finest musicians. He anticipated becoming the conductor of a major orchestra, and he was granted the podium of Leipzig's prestigious Gewandhaus Orchestra.

His positive expectations extended beyond his musicianship and into his personal life. He enjoyed a wealth of fine friends, including some of the greatest composers of his day. And, yes, Mendelssohn was blessed with a wonderful, loving marriage.

In Jesus' Prodigal Son story, the father figure is usually tied to the role of God—eagerly awaiting a wandering child's homecoming. But each of us can learn a lesson from that father—and from Mendelssohn—to expect the best.

PATRICK KAVANAUGH

Ever since I heard about your faith in the Lord Jesus and your love for all the saints, I have not stopped giving thanks for you, remembering you in my prayers.... I pray also that the eyes of your heart may be enlightened in order that you may know the hope to which he has called you, the riches of his glorious inheritance in the saints, and his incomparably great power for us who believe.

EPHESIANS 1:15–16, 18–19

Delight yourself in the LORD

and he will give you the desires of your heart.

Psalm 37:4

Praise be to the God and Father of our Lord Jesus Christ!
In his great mercy he has given us new birth into a living
hope through the resurrection of Jesus Christ from the
dead, and into an inheritance that can never perish, spoil
or fade—kept in heaven for you.

1 Peter 1:3–4

There is surely a future hope for you,
and your hope will not be cut off.

Proverbs 23:18

Jesus said, "Ask and it will be given to you; seek and you will find; knock and the door will be opened to you. For everyone who asks receives; he who seeks finds; and to him who knocks, the door will be opened."

Matthew 7:7–8

He who did not spare his own Son, but gave him up for us all — how will he not also, along with him, graciously give us all things?

Romans 8:32

You also were included in Christ when you heard the word of truth, the gospel of your salvation. Having believed, you were marked in him with a seal, the promised Holy Spirit, who is a deposit guaranteeing our inheritance until the redemption of those who are God's possession—to the praise of his glory.

Ephesians 1:13–14

Commit to the LORD whatever you do, and your plans will succeed.

Proverbs 16:3

Jesus said, "Ask and you will receive, and your joy will be complete."

John 16:24

Hope does not disappoint us, because God has poured out his love into our hearts by the Holy Spirit, whom he has given us.

Romans 5:5

We wait for the blessed hope—the glorious appearing of our great God and Savior, Jesus Christ.

Titus 2:13

Set your hope fully on the grace to be given you when Jesus Christ is revealed.

1 Peter 1:13

A longing fulfilled is a tree of life.

Proverbs 13:12

Excellence

*We are God's workmanship, created in Christ Jesus to do
good works, which God prepared in advance for us to do.*

EPHESIANS 2:10

I smile when I read these lines from a George Eliot poem titled
"Stradivarius":

> 'Tis God gives skill,
> But not without men's hands;
> He could not make
> Antonio Stradivari's violins
> Without Antonio.

The great Antonio Stradivarius was the world's most celebrated
maker of stringed instruments—violins, violas, cellos, and basses.

Long before names such as Rolls Royce or Hilton bespoke quality,
Stradivarius was a synonym for superior craftsmanship. Even now "a
Stradivarius" is a descriptive noun describing an excellent product. A
sales rep might refer to "the Stradivarius of new cars" or "the
Stradivarius of personal computers."

What is it that makes a Stradivarius violin so magnificent? What
was the great secret that hundreds of experts have tried unsuccess-
fully to copy?

Entire books, some including the most precise technical details,
have been written on this subject. Whatever scientific answers there
may be, all the experts agree on the extraordinary amount of care that
went into each instrument. No sloppiness, no careless corner
cutting—ever.

(continued)

It's a standard of quality that is nearly too high to aim for.

Go back and read again the lighthearted lines in the George Eliot poem and ask yourself one question: Does God need me and my best effort to carry out His most excellent work?

Throughout history God has chosen to use mortal men and women—"jars of clay"—to do His perfect work. He made Antonio's hands—and yours. What excellent work does He ask you to do with them—today?

PATRICK KAVANAUGH

Developing our God-given gifts and talents will only lead to greatness in God's kingdom if we put Jesus at the center of our lives and not our own pride and ambition. Eric Liddell, for example, used his gifts for God's glory and not his own, and God chose to exalt him. Martin Luther King, Jr., found greatness in serving God and proclaiming justice. Mother Teresa found greatness in serving the poor. Even the apostle Paul, the greatest evangelist who ever lived, humbled himself and made himself a servant. And all of them were doing what God had gifted them to do, and all of them loved what they did.

Becoming God's servant is the only greatness we should aspire to, and in the end it will be the most fulfilling and enriching "success story" we can imagine: "And God raised us up with Christ and seated us with him in the heavenly realms in Christ Jesus, in order that in the coming ages he might show the incomparable riches of his grace, expressed in his kindness to us in Christ Jesus. For it is by grace you have been saved, through faith—and this not from yourselves, it is the gift of God" (Ephesians 2:6–9).

LARRY BAUER

Whatever you do, work at it with all your heart, as working for the Lord, not for men, since you know that you will receive an inheritance from the Lord as a reward. It is the Lord Christ you are serving.

Colossians 3:23–24

I praise you because I am fearfully
and wonderfully made;
your works are wonderful,
I know that full well.

Psalm 139:14

*God is able to make all grace
abound to you, so that in all
things at all times, having all
that you need, you will
abound in every good work.*

2 Corinthians 9:8

Whatever is true, whatever is noble,
whatever is right, whatever is pure,
whatever is lovely, whatever is
admirable—if anything is excellent or
praiseworthy—think about such
things.

Philippians 4:8

Just as you excel in everything—in
faith, in speech, in knowledge, in complete earnestness and in your love for
us—see that you also excel in this
grace of giving.

2 Corinthians 8:7

*Whatever you do, do it all for
the glory of God.*

1 Corinthians 10:31

Now I will show you the most excellent way.
   If I speak in the tongues of men
and of angels, but have not love, I am
only a resounding gong or a clanging
cymbal. If I have the gift of prophecy
and can fathom all mysteries and all
knowledge, and if I have a faith that
can move mountains, but have not
love, I am nothing. If I give all I
possess to the poor and surrender my
body to the flames, but have not love,
I gain nothing.
   Love is patient, love is kind. It does
not envy, it does not boast, it is not
proud. It is not rude, it is not self-
seeking, it is not easily angered, it
keeps no record of wrongs. Love does
not delight in evil but rejoices with the
truth. It always protects, always trusts,
always hopes, always perseveres.
Love never fails.

1 Corinthians 12:31–13:8

FOCUS

"Be still, and know that I am God; I will be exalted among the nations, I will be exalted in the earth."

PSALM 46:10

If there is one topic that I delight in meditating upon repeatedly, it is...the unfailing love of God. Nothing so comforts me, so steadies me, so nourishes me as the truth of God's unfailing love for his people....

I would like to suggest a spiritual exercise that I believe can revolutionize your knowledge of God and your relationship with him. The concept is expressed in the oldest psalm of the Bible, penned by Moses: "Satisfy us in the morning with your unfailing love, that we may sing for joy and be glad all our days" (Psalm 90:14).

Each morning, think upon God's unfailing love, how it is expressed to you, its immensity, its power, its nature. Let God satisfy you with the sure knowledge that he has set his love upon you and will never turn it away. The more frequently you ponder God's boundless love, the more joyful you will become. The more joyful you are, the more exciting is your walk with Jesus and the more dynamic is your faith.

The unfailing, steadfast love of Christ for you is your anchor for every storm, sustaining you, keeping you, upholding you. It satisfies the deepest longing of your heart.

CHARLES STANLEY

I will sing of the LORD's great love forever;

   with my mouth I will make your faithfulness known through

      all generations.

I will declare that your love stands firm forever,

   that you established your faithfulness in heaven itself....

In the council of the holy ones God is greatly feared;

   he is more awesome than all who surround him.

O LORD God Almighty, who is like you?

   You are mighty, O LORD, and your faithfulness surrounds you.

PSALM 89:1–2, 7–8

One day I came home from work immensely discouraged by the events of the day. Then I read Philippians. The call to prayer impressed me. "Do not be anxious about anything, but in everything, by prayer and petition, with thanksgiving, present your requests to God. And the peace of God, which transcends all understanding, will guard your hearts and your minds in Christ Jesus" (4:6–7).

What struck me was the phrase "with thanksgiving." I decided to take the phrase literally. I began thanking God for all the material things in my bedroom—the bed, the box springs, the mattress. I thanked God for everything in one room. In the process of this simple exercise, something supernatural happened. The despair faded into insignificance, and I was overwhelmed by the goodness of God. And this was just one room of our home. I did not get to the other rooms. I did not get to the spiritual blessings that are far more significant than the material ones.

Christians can face the greatest despair with a spirit of faith. Jesus is alive! We will be raised with him in the great resurrection! We are recipients of the overflowing grace of God! We have much for which to be thankful.

EDWARD G. DOBSON

So we fix our eyes not on what is seen, but on what is unseen. For what is seen is temporary, but what is unseen is eternal.

2 Corinthians 4:18

I have set the LORD always before me.
  Because he is at my right hand,
  I will not be shaken.

Psalm 16:8

Devote yourselves to prayer, being watchful and thankful.

Colossians 4:2

I will extol the LORD at all times;
  his praise will always be on my lips.

Psalm 34:1

Teach us to number our days aright,
  that we may gain a heart of wisdom.

Psalm 90:12

Fix these words of mine in your hearts
and minds; tie them as symbols on
your hands and bind them on your
foreheads.

Deuteronomy 11:18

Live in a right way in undivided devotion to the Lord.

1 Corinthians 7:35

Let your eyes look straight ahead,
  fix your gaze directly before you.
Make level paths for your feet
  and take only ways that are firm.

Proverbs 4:25–26

Fear the LORD and serve him faithfully with all your heart; consider what great things he has done for you.

1 Samuel 12:24

"You will seek me and find me when
you seek me with all your heart. I will
be found by you," declares the LORD.

Jeremiah 29:13–14

Fix your thoughts on Jesus, the apostle and high priest whom we confess.

Hebrews 3:1

IMAGINATION

The heavens declare the glory of God;
   the skies proclaim the work of his hands.

PSALM 19:1

God created the universe! He created the stars! The heavens! He created the Grand Canyon! Niagara Falls! The Alps! All that is spectacular, God has created. But we can easily forget that God also created the single blade of grass and the smallest piece of dust that floats in the sunlight of your room.

We should not forget that God is the Creator of all things great and small.

Do you remember the delight you felt after you created something: a flower arrangement, a painting, a garden, a baby, a report, a song? Can you imagine the delight God must have felt after He created the sun, the moon, the earth and all its treasures? Can you imagine how pleased He was when He created you?

God the artist. God the craftsman. God the maker. Walk through the day as if you are visiting an art gallery and take delight in all that you see framed in heaven's gold.

CHRISTOPHER DE VINCK

Artists look at things differently than nonartists do. We notice detail; we appreciate nuance and beauty. Some people might look at the evening sky and all they see is a bunch of stars. But an artist looks at it and sees beauty and meaning. Artists want to sit under the stars and soak it all in. They want to gaze at the moon and be dazzled. They want to paint a picture of it or write a song or a poem.

Debussy was so moved by the evening sky that he wrote *Clair de Lune*. Van Gogh was inspired and painted *Starry Night*. King David was an artist who looked at the evening sky and wrote this: "When I consider your heavens, the work of your fingers, the moon and the stars, which you have set in place, what is man that you are mindful of him, the son of man that you care for him?" (Ps. 8:3–4)....

In *Windows of the Soul* Ken Gire writes, "We learn from the artists, from those who work in paint or words, or musical notes, from those who have eyes that see and ears that hear and hearts that feel deeply and passionately about all that is sacred and dear to God."

RORY NOLAND

Praise the LORD from the heavens,
  praise him in the heights above.
Praise him, all his angels,
  praise him, all his heavenly hosts.
Praise him, sun and moon,
  praise him, all you shining stars.
Praise him, you highest heavens
  and you waters above the skies.
Let them praise the name of the LORD,
  for he commanded and they were created.
He set them in place for ever and ever;
  he gave a decree that will never pass away.

PSALM 148:1–6

Lift your eyes and look to the heavens:
  Who created all these?
He who brings out the starry host one by one,
  and calls them each by name.
Because of his great power and mighty strength,
  not one of them is missing.

Isaiah 40:26

"My thoughts are not your thoughts,
  neither are your ways my ways," declares the LORD.
"As the heavens are higher than the earth,
  so are my ways higher than your ways
  and my thoughts than your thoughts."

Isaiah 55:8–9

Sing to the LORD a new song;
  sing to the LORD, all the earth.
Sing to the LORD, praise his name;
  proclaim his salvation day after day.
Declare his glory among the nations,
  his marvelous deeds among all peoples.

Psalm 96:1–3

How precious to me are your thoughts,
 O God!
 How vast is the sum of them!
Were I to count them,
 they would outnumber the grains
 of sand.

Psalm 139:17–18

No eye has seen, no ear has heard, no mind has conceived what God has prepared for those who love him.

1 Corinthians 2:9

I will remember the deeds of the LORD;
 yes, I will remember your miracles
 of long ago.
I will meditate on all your works
 and consider all your mighty deeds.

Psalm 77:11–12

To him who is able to do immeasurably more than all we ask or imagine, according to his power that is at work within us, to him be glory in the church and in Christ Jesus throughout all generations, for ever and ever!

Ephesians 3:20–21

We, who with unveiled faces all reflect the Lord's glory, are being transformed into his likeness with ever-increasing glory, which comes from the Lord, who is the Spirit.

2 Corinthians 3:18

"I will pour out my Spirit on all people.
Your sons and daughters will prophesy,
 your old men will dream dreams,
 your young men will see visions."

Joel 2:28

Now we see but a poor reflection as in a mirror; then we shall see face to face. Now I know in part; then I shall know fully, even as I am fully known.

1 Corinthians 13:12

Look at the nations and watch—
 and be utterly amazed.
For I am going to do something in
 your days
 that you would not believe,
 even if you were told.

Habakkuk 1:5

INITIATIVE

Never be lacking in zeal, but keep your spiritual fervor, serving the Lord. Be joyful in hope, patient in affliction, faithful in prayer.

ROMANS 12:11–12

Bernard of Clairvaux was born in Fontaines, France, around the year 1090. No one expected much of this frail child, who in time was deemed too weak to serve in the military.

Devoted to his Lord, the young man entered a monastery. Here, he might have buried himself along with thousands of other young monks in the Middle Ages, never to be remembered in the annals of history. But God had a great task for this weak boy.

In the monastery, Bernard's superiors noticed his enthusiasm and ability to motivate his fellow monks into greater love of Jesus. Within three years of his arrival, Bernard was sent out to found and ordain the new monastery of Clairvaux. Could this weakling possibly succeed in such a daunting task?

With zeal and faith as his primary resources, Bernard launched the enterprise. His spirited preaching proved popular among the country people. Before long, dozens of men came knocking on his door, committing their lives to the service of Christ. The Clairvaux monastery, of which Bernard was abbot until his death in 1153, became well-known throughout all of Christendom as a bastion of Christian faith and ministry....

(continued)

How can this be, that such a hopeless failure with little promise became God's messenger to an entire generation? There were surely young men nearby with more talent, more education, more of a "future." Yet Bernard had something that most of his contemporaries lacked: an unquenchable love for God and an enthusiasm that motivated his own service and the service of others. This was the key to his monastery, his life, and his powerful ministry.

PATRICK KAVANAUGH

Scripture specifically states God's will for each of us. The power of this truth motivates and energizes us and adds creativity and excitement to any endeavor. It can pull us out of bed in the morning with renewed enthusiasm. It tells us when we're in the center of God's will, gives us a sense of purpose, and adds to our self-worth. It can even help us find, or live successfully with, our mate.

What is God's will? A lawyer once asked Jesus that same question. Jesus told him that God's highest will, the greatest commandment, was to "Love the Lord your God with all your heart, and with all your soul, and with all your mind" (Matthew 22:37). Then he added the second greatest commandment: "Love your neighbor as yourself" (Matthew 22:39). That pretty well covers it all; everything else required by God flows from these two commandments.

Obedience to the first commandment fills us; obedience to the second makes us overflow with motivation, creativity, and excitement about life.

GARY SMALLEY

Fight the good fight of the faith. Take hold of the eternal life to which you were called when you made your good confession in the presence of many witnesses.

1 Timothy 6:12

Though you have not seen him, you love him; and even though you do not see him now, you believe in him and are filled with an inexpressible and glorious joy, for you are receiving the goal of your faith, the salvation of your souls.

1 Peter 1:8–9

"My food," said Jesus, "is to do the will of him who sent me and to finish his work."

John 4:34

Whatever your hand finds to do, do it with all your might.

Ecclesiastes 9:10

Always give yourselves fully to the work of the Lord, because you know that your labor in the Lord is not in vain.

1 Corinthians 15:58

Nothing is better for a man under the sun than to eat and drink and be glad. Then joy will accompany him in his work all the days of the life God has given him under the sun.

Ecclesiastes 8:15

We rebuilt the wall till all of it reached half its height, for the people worked with all their heart.

Nehemiah 4:6

We continually remember before our God and Father your work produced by faith, your labor prompted by love, and your endurance inspired by hope in our Lord Jesus Christ.

1 Thessalonians 1:3

We have different gifts, according to the grace given us. If a man's gift is prophesying, let him use it in proportion to his faith. If it is serving, let him serve; if it is teaching, let him teach; if it is encouraging, let him encourage; if it is contributing to the needs of others, let him give generously; if it is leadership, let him govern diligently; if it is showing mercy, let him do it cheerfully.

Romans 12:6–8

Acknowledge the God of your father, and serve him with wholehearted devotion and with a willing mind.

1 Chronicles 28:9

Finish the work, so that your eager willingness to do it may be matched by your completion of it.

2 Corinthians 8:11

INNOVATION

"Forget the former things; do not dwell on the past.
See, I am doing a new thing!"

ISAIAH 43:18–19

Why do you cut off the ends of a roast before cooking it?" a husband asked his wife.

"Because my mother did it that way," she responded with a smile.

Curious, the husband called his wife's mother and asked her the same question. When she gave an identical answer, he called his wife's grandmother. The moment the elderly matron heard the question she laughed and said, "I don't know why they cut off the ends of the roast, but I did it that way because a full roast wouldn't fit into my pan."

That story illustrates how most practices are initiated to serve a purpose. But over time, even the best practice can lose its usefulness. It takes a wise leader to know when to change something. It takes insight to recognize when it's time for innovation. Jesus certainly understood the role of change and rebuked those who stood in the way of innovation.

The Pharisees chided Jesus because he didn't force his disciples to fast (Mark 2:18). The Lord made it clear to the religious leaders that he hadn't come to patch an old system (vv. 21–22).

Such an effort would be as foolish as putting a patch of unshrunk cloth on an old garment, or putting new wine in an old wineskin. When the patch shrunk, the garment would tear. When the wine fermented, the wineskin would burst. The old forms of Judaism could never contain the spirit of Jesus' message.

Jesus was an innovator. A change maker. And so is every effective leader.

THE LEADERSHIP BIBLE,
NEW INTERNATIONAL VERSION

In their excellent book *Built to Last*, James C. Collins and Jerry L. Porras note that, once a visionary company identifies its core ideology, it preserves it almost religiously—changing it seldom, if ever. These authors conclude that "core values in a visionary company form a rock-solid foundation and do not drift with the trends and fashions of the day. In some cases, the core values have remained intact for well over one hundred years. Yet, while keeping their core ideologies tightly fixed, visionary companies display a powerful desire for progress that enables them to change and adapt without compromising their cherished core ideals."

Paul had his itinerary and his maps. "Bithynia or Bust" was written on the side of his donkey. But God changed this to "Macedonia or Bust!" Change—new direction. But Paul's core value was not Bithynia. It was fulfilling God's desire to expand his kingdom. Because he didn't confuse his desire (to go to Bithynia) with his core value (to follow God's call), Paul enthusiastically "sailed straight for Samothrace" (Acts 16:11). Like Paul, all godly leaders need the ability to hold to core values while making those changes necessary to advance their cause.

THE LEADERSHIP BIBLE,
NEW INTERNATIONAL VERSION

"The time is coming," declares the LORD,

    "when I will make a new covenant

with the house of Israel

    and with the house of Judah.

It will not be like the covenant

    I made with their forefathers

when I took them by the hand

    to lead them out of Egypt,

because they broke my covenant,

    though I was a husband to them,"

        declares the LORD.

"This is the covenant I will make with the house of Israel

    after that time," declares the LORD.

"I will put my law in their minds

    and write it on their hearts.

I will be their God,

    and they will be my people.

No longer will a man teach his neighbor,

    or a man his brother, saying, 'Know the LORD,'

because they will all know me,

    from the least of them to the greatest,"

        declares the LORD.

"For I will forgive their wickedness

    and will remember their sins no more."

Jeremiah 31:31–34

You show that you are a letter from Christ...written not with ink but with the Spirit of the living God, not on tablets of stone but on tablets of human hearts.

2 Corinthians 3:3

Sing to the LORD a new song,
    for he has done marvelous things;
his right hand and his holy arm
    have worked salvation for him.
The LORD has made his salvation
      known
    and revealed his righteousness
      to the nations.
He has remembered his love
    and his faithfulness to the house
      of Israel;
all the ends of the earth have seen
    the salvation of our God.

Psalm 98:1–3

He has made us competent as ministers of a new covenant—not of the letter but of the Spirit; for the letter kills, but the Spirit gives life.

2 Corinthians 3:6

The Lord Jesus, on the night he was betrayed, took bread, and when he had given thanks, he broke it and said, "This is my body, which is for you; do this in remembrance of me." In the same way, after supper he took the cup, saying, "This cup is the new covenant in my blood; do this, whenever you drink it, in remembrance of me."

1 Corinthians 11:23–25

INTEGRITY

Commit your way to the LORD;
trust in him and he will do this:
He will make your righteousness shine like the dawn,
the justice of your cause like the noonday sun.

PSALM 37:5–6

Joseph found himself in an enticing situation. Potiphar had fully trusted Joseph and had put him in charge of all of his household. But now Potiphar's wife was making a pass at the young Hebrew....

Joseph, however, realized that even though he might "get away" with the affair, he would still be sinning against God. Joseph knew that nothing he had ever done, whether good or bad, had escaped the eyes of the Lord, and that reality gave him perspective. Joseph resolved in his heart that he would maintain purity in this situation even though "she spoke to Joseph day after day" (Genesis 39:10). Not only did Joseph refuse to go to bed with her, he refused even to be in the same room with her! He firmly put his desire to please and to serve God above any of his own sinful cravings.

We can learn a lot from Joseph's example. It seems clear that he had made a commitment to purity long before he found himself in a tempting situation. He had decided what his boundaries were. So when the tempting situation presented itself, he was able to turn away from it without hesitation. Purity began in Joseph's heart and mind—before he was tempted—and he was ready to make purity a verb.

(continued)

How would each of us react in Joseph's situation? If we make a decision to live purely—thinking through and setting boundaries for our behavior before we encounter temptation—and then ask God to provide us with the strength to stick to it, we are ready to face those tempting situations when no one is looking.

STEVE RUGG

How do you spell success? The culture we live in spells it academic achievement, money, fame, popularity or security. Success is when we get that scholastic prize, buy the big house, sell our paintings in a high-end gallery, or make it on Wall Street. The emphasis is on the end result of all of our work and ambition. It becomes a problem when we give so much significance to the goal that we tend to get there by any means we can: If we're happy with the end result, who cares about ethics or morals or integrity? If I get an A on an exam, does it matter whether I did the work myself? As long as nobody gets hurt, does it make a difference if I lie a little to get the job?

In God's definition of success, the means and the end are synonymous. God is concerned with the end results of our living and working; he wants us to become successful in what he gives us to do. But he is also concerned about the means: he wants us to prosper by loving him, talking to him and delighting in his Word.

KENT WALSTROM

Jesus said, "Whoever acknowledges me before men, I will also acknowledge him before my Father in heaven."

Matthew 10:32

LORD, who may dwell in your sanctuary?
　　Who may live on your holy hill?
He whose walk is blameless
　　and who does what is righteous,
who speaks the truth from his heart
　　and has no slander on his tongue,
who does his neighbor no wrong
　　and casts no slur on his fellowman,
who despises a vile man
　　but honors those who fear the LORD,
who keeps his oath
　　even when it hurts,
who lends his money without usury
　　and does not accept a bribe against the innocent.
He who does these things
　　will never be shaken.

Psalm 15

Create in me a pure heart, O God,
　　and renew a steadfast spirit within me.

Psalm 51:10

May the words of my mouth and the
　　meditation of my heart
be pleasing in your sight,
O LORD, my Rock and my
　　Redeemer.

Psalm 19:14

Jesus said, "You are the light of the
world. A city on a hill cannot be
hidden. Neither do people light a
lamp and put it under a bowl. Instead
they put it on its stand, and it gives
light to everyone in the house. In the
same way, let your light shine before
men, that they may see your good
deeds and praise your Father
in heaven."

Matthew 5:14–16

The LORD watches over the way of the righteous.

Psalm 1:6

Surely, O LORD you bless the
　　righteous;
　you surround them with your
　　favor as with a shield.

Psalm 5:12

The righteous will inherit the land
　　and dwell in it forever.

Psalm 37:29

Light is shed upon the righteous
　　and joy on the upright in heart.

Psalm 97:11

I know, my God, that you test the heart and are pleased with integrity.

1 Chronicles 29:17

In righteousness I will see your face;
　　when I awake, I will be satisfied
　　　with seeing your likeness.

Psalm 17:15

Test me, O Lord, and try me,
　　examine my heart and my mind;
for your love is ever before me,
　　and I walk continually in your truth.

Psalm 26:2–3

LEADERSHIP

Be shepherds of God's flock that is under your care, serving as overseers — not because you must, but because you are willing, as God wants you to be; not greedy for money, but eager to serve; not lording it over those entrusted to you, but being examples to the flock. And when the Chief Shepherd appears, you will receive the crown of glory that will never fade away.

1 PETER 5:2–4

What is it about some leaders? They seem to have that extra "Oomph!" Their people are unusually productive, grievances from their area are infrequent and quality is high. People from other areas want to be transferred to their departments. The secret? Passion! Enthusiasm! These leaders have a clearly defined purpose that transcends merely pushing product out the door.

Caleb was that kind of leader. His "secret" was a secret to no one. Three times his brief biography states that Caleb "followed the LORD...wholeheartedly" (Joshua 14:8, 9, 14). He was enthusiastic, gutsy, passionate about proving what the Lord could do through one who trusted him completely.

Passion and clear purpose served Caleb well for his many years. And these two qualities are still an essential part of great leadership. For Caleb, that purpose and its consequent passion were transcendent. They were greater than any product of promotion or profit. He found a life-consuming passion: "I followed the LORD my God wholeheartedly." No higher purpose and no greater passion exist. This purpose gives maximum meaning to whatever a leader does.

THE LEADERSHIP BIBLE,
NEW INTERNATIONAL VERSION

The LORD is my shepherd, I shall not be in want.

He makes me lie down in green pastures,

he leads me beside quiet waters,

he restores my soul.

He guides me in paths of righteousness

for his name's sake.

Even though I walk

through the valley of the shadow of death,

I will fear no evil,

for you are with me;

your rod and your staff,

they comfort me.

PSALM 23:1–4

The most effective leaders are servants. Nobody demonstrated this better than Jesus on the night prior to his crucifixion. Alone with his disciples in a room in Jerusalem, Jesus did the unthinkable. When there was no servant to carry out the custom of foot washing, Jesus assumed the role. The Master became the servant. The greatest and most high became the least and the lowest.

Jesus was able to do this because he was secure in himself. He knew who he was and where he was going (John 13:1). But Jesus also served his disciples because he loved them (v. 1). While these two reasons would be adequate in and of themselves, the Lord had another reason for his actions. When he had finished washing the disciples' feet, Jesus told them, "I have set you an example that you should do as I have done for you" (v. 15). The Lord didn't tell them to do "what" he had done. He commanded them to do "as" he had done. They weren't to become full-time footwashers, but rather full-time servers of men and women. They were to be servant leaders.

THE LEADERSHIP BIBLE,
NEW INTERNATIONAL VERSION

Jesus said, "I am the good shepherd. The good shepherd lays down his life for the sheep. The hired hand is not the shepherd who owns the sheep. So when he sees the wolf coming, he abandons the sheep and runs away. Then the wolf attacks the flock and scatters it. The man runs away because he is a hired hand and cares nothing for the sheep. I am the good shepherd; I know my sheep and my sheep know me—just as the Father knows me and I know the Father—and I lay down my life for the sheep."

John 10:11–15

Jesus said, "From everyone who has been given much, much will be demanded; and from the one who has been entrusted with much, much more will be asked."

Luke 12:48

Teach what is in accord with sound doctrine. Teach the older men to be temperate, worthy of respect, self-controlled, and sound in faith, in love and in endurance. Likewise, teach the older women to be reverent in the way they live, not to be slanderers or addicted to much wine, but to teach what is good. Then they can train the younger women to love their husbands and children, to be self-controlled and pure, to be busy at home, to be kind, and to be subject to their husbands, so that no one will malign the word of God. Similarly, encourage the young men to be self-controlled. In everything set them an example by doing what is good. In your teaching show integrity, seriousness and soundness of speech.

Titus 2:1–8

Don't let anyone look down on you because you are young, but set an example for the believers in speech, in life, in love, in faith and in purity. Until I come, devote yourself to the public reading of Scripture, to preaching and to teaching. Do not neglect your gift, which was given you through a prophetic message when the body of elders laid their hands on you. Be diligent in these matters; give yourself wholly to them, so that everyone may see your progress. Watch your life and doctrine closely. Persevere in them, because if you do, you will save both yourself and your hearers.

I Timothy 4:12–16

The Lamb at the center of the throne will be their shepherd; he will lead them to springs of living water.

Revelation 7:17

Not many of you should presume to be teachers, my brothers, because you know that we who teach will be judged more strictly.

James 3:1

PERSEVERANCE

Do you not know that in a race all the runners run, but only one gets the prize? Run in such a way as to get the prize. Everyone who competes in the games goes into strict training. They do it to get a crown that will not last; but we do it to get a crown that will last forever.

1 CORINTHIANS 9:24–25

I was embarrassed—so much so that I kept avoiding my turn in the rotation. Every guy my age in the weight room was bench-pressing at least 115 pounds. At my best, I could lift only 85 pounds. "I'll never be able to catch up," I thought. The standard was just too high.

Then the thought occurred to me that I probably couldn't make up a 30-pound difference overnight, but I could work on five pounds at a time. So I began the slow process of lowering the weight bar to 90 pounds and working hard until I could easily lift it.

Success! I pressed 90 pounds, then raised my goal to 95. It was hard work, but after awhile I reached that goal too. I was motivated to raise my goal again, and again, and again. After months of inching my way along, little by little, I found that I was bench-pressing 200 pounds! All those seemingly insignificant increments added up over time.

Our growth as Christians is also incremental. Like adding weight to a bench press, we are to "make every effort to add to [our] faith goodness; and to goodness, knowledge; and to knowledge, self-control; and to self-control, perseverance; and to perseverance, god-liness; and to godliness, brotherly kindness; and to brotherly kind-ness, love. For if you possess these qualities in increasing measure, they will keep you from being ineffective and unproductive in your knowledge of our Lord Jesus Christ" (2 Peter 1:5–8).

TERRY COOK

Noah had to wait a long time before he saw God act. From the time Noah was given the promise concerning the flood, until the rain began to fall, perhaps as many as one hundred and twenty years had elapsed (compare Genesis 5:32; 6:3 and 7:6). From the time the rain started until his family left the ark, Noah waited another year inside the closed ark (compare Genesis 7:11 and 8:14). As Noah waited those many years for the first raindrops to fall, it's very likely he was subject to times of doubt. But he remained obedient to all God had told him (Genesis 7:5). God had promised, and Noah took him at his word. It was not a matter of if, but when....

What answers to prayer are you waiting for? Does God seem to take intolerably long to show you that he has heard? Don't give up. God will answer in his perfect timing. "You need to persevere so that when you have done the will of God, you will receive what he has promised" (Hebrews 10:36).

TOM YEAKLEY

Blessed is the man who perseveres under trial, because when he has stood the test, he will receive the crown of life that God has promised to those who love him.

James 1:12

I press on to take hold of that for which Christ Jesus took hold of me. Brothers, I do not consider myself yet to have taken hold of it. But one thing I do: Forgetting what is behind and straining toward what is ahead, I press on toward the goal to win the prize for which God has called me heavenward in Christ Jesus.

Philippians 3:12–14

May the Lord direct your hearts into God's love and Christ's perseverance.

2 Thessalonians 3:5

Let us throw off everything that hinders and the sin that so easily entangles, and let us run with perseverance the race marked out for us.

Hebrews 12:1

I have fought the good fight, I have finished the race, I have kept the faith. Now there is in store for me the crown of righteousness, which the Lord, the righteous Judge, will award to me on that day—and not only to me, but also to all who have longed for his appearing.

2 Timothy 4:7–8

Consider it pure joy, my brothers, whenever you face trials of many kinds, because you know that the testing of your faith develops perseverance. Perseverance must finish its work so that you may be mature and complete, not lacking anything.

James 1:2–4

Everyone born of God overcomes the world. This is the victory that has overcome the world, even our faith.

1 John 5:4

Jesus said, "To him who overcomes, I will give the right to sit with me on my throne, just as I overcame and sat down with my Father on his throne."

Revelation 3:21

Jesus said, "In this world you will have trouble. But take heart! I have overcome the world."

John 16:33

God "will give to each person according to what he has done." To those who by persistence in doing good seek glory, honor and immortality, he will give eternal life.

Romans 2:6–7

PRIORITIES

We fix our eyes not on what is seen, but on what is unseen.
For what is seen is temporary, but what is unseen is eternal.

2 CORINTHIANS 4:17–18

One day when the human race had not heard a word of hope for a long time, a man named Moses walked past a shrub. He had seen it before, perhaps a hundred times. Only this time it was different.... This time the bush is on fire with the presence of God.

And Moses said, "I must turn aside and look at this great sight, and see why the bush is not burned up." Everything turned on Moses' being willing to "turn aside"—to interrupt his daily routine to pay attention to the presence of God. He didn't have to. He could have looked the other way, as many of us would. He would have just missed the Exodus, the people of Israel, his calling, the reason for his existence. He would have missed knowing God....

For a long time in my own life a very bad thing happened: I had reduced my "tools for spiritual growth" to a few activities such as prayer and Bible study or a few periods of the day called a quiet time. I took an embarrassingly long time to learn that every moment of my life is an opportunity to learn from God how to live like Jesus, how to live in the kingdom of God. I had to discover that there are practical, concrete ways to help me "turn aside."

Elizabeth Barrett Browning wrote:

> Earth's crammed with Heaven,
> And every common bush afire with God,
> But only he who sees takes off his shoes—
> The rest sit round it and pluck blackberries.

JOHN ORTBERG

Susan Yates, a popular author and family-conference speaker, tells the story of how she learned to reorder her priorities and be more generous with her time. One evening, as Susan confronted a stack of unpaid bills, one of her daughters asked for a back rub before bed. Susan decided to tackle the bills first, as the job had been on her "to do" list all day. But by the time she sealed the last envelope and made her way upstairs to her daughter's room, the girl was fast asleep.

A few days later, Susan's son announced he had a school report to do on Abraham Lincoln. He wanted her to drive him to the nearby Lincoln Memorial so he could get some "inspiration." This time, instead of putting her own schedule and desires at the top of the priority list, she put her son first. The two of them spent a couple of hours walking around the Lincoln Memorial, talking the whole time. The experience might not have helped the school report, but today it stands out in Susan's mind as an instance of time well spent.

RON BLUE

Hold on to instruction, do not let it go;

guard it well, for it is your life.

Proverbs 4:13

Come, all you who are thirsty,

come to the waters;

and you who have no money,

come, buy and eat!

Come, buy wine and milk

without money and without cost.

Why spend money on what is not bread,

and your labor on what does not satisfy?

Listen, listen to me, and eat what is good,

and your soul will delight in the richest of fare.

Isaiah 55:1–2

Above all else, guard your heart,
for it is the wellspring of life.

Proverbs 4:23

Jesus said, "Do not work for food that spoils, but for food that endures to eternal life, which the Son of Man will give you."

John 6:27

Jesus said, "No one can serve two masters. Either he will hate the one and love the other, or he will be devoted to the one and despise the other. You cannot serve both God and Money."

Matthew 6:24

I have set before you life and death, blessings and curses. Now choose life, so that you and your children may live and that you may love the LORD your God, listen to his voice, and hold fast to him. For the LORD is your life.

Deuteronomy 30:19–20

Train yourself to be godly. For physical training is of some value, but godliness has value for all things, holding promise for both the present life and the life to come.

1 Timothy 4:7–8

Whoever sows generously will also reap generously. Each man should give what he has decided in his heart to give, not reluctantly or under compulsion, for God loves a cheerful giver.

2 Corinthians 9:6–7

"Bring the whole tithe into the storehouse, that there may be food in my house. Test me in this," says the LORD Almighty, "and see if I will not throw open the floodgates of heaven and pour out so much blessing that you will not have room enough for it."

Malachi 3:10

The world and its desires pass away, but the man who does the will of God lives forever.

1 John 2:17

RESPECT

Make it your ambition to lead a quiet life, to mind your own business and to work with your hands, just as we told you, so that your daily life may win the respect of outsiders and so that you will not be dependent on anybody.

I THESSALONIANS 4:11,12

God offered us His love without considering whether we deserved it or not; we are called to offer love in exactly the same way. Or, in the words of Paul, "in humility consider others more important than yourselves." Can you think of any idea more opposed to the Pecking Order? Can you imagine the implications of actually applying that notion to real life?...

Think about society. Can you imagine what would happen in the marketplace if everybody in the company treated everybody else like a VIP? If officers treated clerical workers the same; if presidents showed honor and respect to night janitors?...

Think about our marriages. What if a husband stopped viewing himself as "Chicken Number One," who has the right to peck away at his wife, "Chicken Number Two," who, in retaliation, pecks at the kids, the dog, or a door-to-door salesman.

Can you imagine what would happen if each husband said, "My wife is a Very Important Person, and I am going to honor, respect and encourage her." And if the wife said the same thing about her husband?

(continued)

Imagine the impact we could leave on people's lives if we all practiced preferential treatment for everyone? Imagine how we could please God if we went out of our way to show His love to those less fortunate, less privileged, or less powerful than we?...

Consider the life of Jesus Christ. Emptying Himself of His divine right, He humbly descended to earth. With every breath, every word, every action, He defied the Pecking Order. He loved unconditionally.

BILL HYBELS

I knew I based my respect on the wrong thing: competence. No person can be perfectly competent at all times. Thus, my respect for anyone would never last. At that point, I realized that I didn't know what to use as my foundation for respecting others.

Webster defines respect as holding in esteem or honor. What I needed to know was how someone gets to that place of honor. 1 Thessalonians 5:12–13 says you should respect them, and you should hold them in the highest regard. In other words, I learned I must freely give respect to others, instead of expecting them to earn it. They are human beings made in God's image, so I need to honor them as such.

Let me challenge you to think through all your relationships. On what do you base your respect for others: their performance or on grace you freely extend? Thanks be to God that he bases our individual worth not on our performance, but rather on his grace!

CAROL RUGG

God chose the foolish things of the world to shame the wise;
God chose the weak things of the world to shame the strong.
He chose the lowly things of this world and the despised
things—and the things that are not—to nullify the things
that are, so that no one may boast before him.

1 Corinthians 1:27–29

Give everyone what you owe him: If you owe taxes, pay
taxes; if revenue, then revenue; if respect, then respect; if
honor, then honor. Let no debt remain outstanding, except
the continuing debt to love one another, for he who loves his
fellowman has fulfilled the law.

Romans 13:7–8

Jesus said, "In everything, do to others what you would have them do to you, for this sums up the Law and the Prophets."

Matthew 7:12

Live a life worthy of the calling you have received. Be completely humble and gentle; be patient, bearing with one another in love. Make every effort to keep the unity of the Spirit through the bond of peace.

Ephesians 4:1–3

As believers in our glorious Lord Jesus Christ, don't show favoritism.

James 2:1

May the God who gives endurance and encouragement give you a spirit of unity among yourselves as you follow Christ Jesus, so that with one heart and mouth you may glorify the God and Father of our Lord Jesus Christ. Accept one another, then, just as Christ accepted you, in order to bring praise to God.

Romans 15:5–7

Has not God chosen those who are poor in the eyes of the world to be rich in faith and to inherit the kingdom he promised those who love him?

James 2:5

Be devoted to one another in brotherly love. Honor one another above yourselves.

Romans 12:10

If you have any encouragement from being united with Christ, if any comfort from his love, if any fellowship with the Spirit, if any tenderness and compassion, then make my joy complete by being like-minded, having the same love, being one in spirit and purpose. Do nothing out of selfish ambition or vain conceit, but in humility consider others better than yourselves. Each of you should look not only to your own interests, but also to the interests of others.

Philippians 2:1–4

How good and pleasant it is
    when brothers live together in unity!

Psalm 133:1

SERVICE

Those who have served well gain an excellent standing and great assurance in their faith in Christ Jesus.

1 TIMOTHY 3:13

Every job provides an opportunity to serve others in some way. The person on the assembly line in Detroit isn't just building cars; he or she is serving the buyer by providing safe transportation. The job may be boring. But viewed as ministry, it is lifted beyond meaningless repetition. Garbage collecting, even when upgraded by the label "sanitation engineer," is hardly an occupation that "utilizes the skills the worker has and provides opportunities to acquire new skills." But this work is essential— a ministry to individuals and the whole community. Work viewed as a ministry makes a difference. For doing our jobs well becomes a significant way of serving Jesus Christ (Ephesians 6:7).

What is your perspective about work? Do you evaluate your work merely in terms of what it offers you? Or do you evaluate your work in terms of what it enables you to do for others? God's perspective seems clear: work is ministry; work gives you and me opportunities to serve.

LARRY RICHARDS

In the Russian church certain people called poustinikki would devote themselves to a life of prayer. They would withdraw to the desert (poustinia) and live in solitude, but not in isolation. (The Russian word for solitude means "being with everybody.") By custom, "the latch was always off the door" as a sign of availability, according to Tilden Edwards. "The poustinik's priority at any time was his neighbor's need (which might stretch beyond prayer and counsel to physical labor, as at harvest time)."

Sometimes in our work we must be interruptible for tasks that are not on our agenda. Sometimes we must live with the "latch off the door." Sometimes we need to be available to talk or pray with troubled people—people whom we will not be able to "cure" and who can't contribute to our career success.

So that I can practice this, occasionally I will set aside a day off at home to be a "day of secret service," when I am simply available to my family and have no agenda of projects or tasks of my own. The idea is that when my only task is to be available, it is impossible to be interrupted. The goal of the day is simply to serve.

JOHN ORTBERG

SERVE THE LORD

WITH FEAR

AND REJOICE

WITH TREMBLING.

PSALM 2:11

Jesus said, "The King will say to those on his right, 'Come, you who are blessed by my Father; take your inheritance, the kingdom prepared for you since the creation of the world. For I was hungry and you gave me something to eat, I was thirsty and you gave me something to drink, I was a stranger and you invited me in, I needed clothes and you clothed me, I was sick and you looked after me, I was in prison and you came to visit me.' Then the righteous will answer him, 'Lord, when did we see you hungry and feed you, or thirsty and give you something to drink? When did we see you a stranger and invite you in, or needing clothes and clothe you? When did we see you sick or in prison and go to visit you?' The King will reply, 'I tell you the truth, whatever you did for one of the least of these brothers of mine, you did for me.' "

Matthew 25:34–40

Jesus said, "The Son of Man did not come to be served, but to serve."

Matthew 20:28

Jesus said, "Whoever serves me must follow me; and where I am, my servant also will be. My Father will honor the one who serves me."

John 12:26

In a large house there are articles not only of gold and silver, but also of wood and clay; some are for noble purposes and some for ignoble. If a man cleanses himself from the latter, he will be an instrument for noble purposes, made holy, useful to the Master and prepared to do any good work.

2 Timothy 2:20–21

Jesus answered, "It is written: 'Worship the LORD your God and serve him only.'"

Luke 4:8

Offer yourselves to God, as those who have been brought from death to life; and offer the parts of your body to him as instruments of righteousness.

Romans 6:13

Offer your bodies as living sacrifices, holy and pleasing to God—this is your spiritual act of worship.

Romans 12:1

Do you not know that your body is a temple of the Holy Spirit, who is in you, whom you have received from God? You are not your own; you were bought at a price. Therefore honor God with your body.

1 Corinthians 6:19–20

STRENGTH

Be strong in the Lord and in his mighty power.

EPHESIANS 6:10

Caleb had such confidence in God that he wasn't afraid to stand out in the crowd. Caleb was one of twelve spies whom God told Moses to send into the promised land in preparation for Israel's invasion. When they returned, all of the spies agreed on the bounty of the land, but ten of them had taken one look at the formidable inhabitants and had immediately concluded that Israel could not overcome "the giants." As they gave Moses their pessimistic report, Caleb jumped up, crying, "We should go up...we can certainly do it" (Numbers 13:30). His opinion was dismissed, but he didn't let it go at that. As the discouraged ex-slaves planned to return to Egypt, Caleb, now joined by Joshua, tore his clothes and shouted, "If the LORD is pleased with us, he will lead us into that land...and will give it to us" (Numbers 14:8). Caleb and Joshua were standing firm, but they were standing alone.

Where did Caleb's confidence come from? Caleb knew God's track record. God had delivered Israel from Egypt with many signs and wonders. Caleb knew that if God said something it was as good as accomplished.

Like Caleb, we too can dare to be different because we know that we do not stand alone, but that we stand with Christ Jesus, "who is able to do immeasurably more than all we ask or imagine, according to his power that is at work within us" (Ephesians 3:20).

MIKE EDSALL

What kind of power is required to speak a universe into existence? What kind of strength must someone possess to scatter stars into infinite space? How explosive do you have to be to ignite the sun or to sustain its fire? What kind of brute force is required to stack up mountains twenty thousand feet into the air?

Only one force is able to accomplish such a feat: God's power.

Throughout history, when God's people found themselves facing impossible odds, they reminded themselves of God's limitless power. Even Job took comfort by remembering "He stirs up the sea with His power. The thunder of His power who can understand?"

We occasionally need a little reminder of what God can do, especially if things aren't going our way. In Psalm 115:3, the psalmist points out that God can do whatever He pleases. That is the essence of what omnipotence is all about. Omnipotent simply means "all-powerful." God never has to ask permission. His unrestrained, indescribable, infinite power and abilities have no parameters.

BILL HYBELS

The LORD is the everlasting God,

    the Creator of the ends of the earth.

He will not grow tired or weary,

    and his understanding no one can fathom.

He gives strength to the weary

    and increases the power of the weak.

Even youths grow tired and weary,

    and young men stumble and fall;

but those who hope in the LORD

    will renew their strength.

They will soar on wings like eagles;

    they will run and not grow weary,

    they will walk and not be faint.

Isaiah 40:28–31

The LORD your God goes with you; he will never leave you nor forsake you.

Deuteronomy 31:6

I lift up my eyes to the hills—
    where does my help come from?
My help comes from the LORD,
    the Maker of heaven and earth.

Psalm 121:1–2

In repentance and rest is your salvation, in quietness and trust is your strength.

Isaiah 30:15

God has said, "Never will I leave you; never will I forsake you." So we say with confidence, "The Lord is my helper; I will not be afraid."

Hebrews 13:5–6

"Surely I am with you always, to the very end of the age."

Matthew 28:20

I can do everything through him who gives me strength.

Philippians 4:13

God did not give us a spirit of timidity, but a spirit of power, of love and of self-discipline.

2 Timothy 1:7

God is our refuge and strength,
    an ever-present help in trouble.

Psalm 46:1

He said to me, "My grace is sufficient for you, for my power is made perfect in weakness." Therefore I will boast all the more gladly about my weaknesses, so that Christ's power may rest on me. That is why, for Christ's sake, I delight in weaknesses, in insults, in hardships, in persecutions, in difficulties. For when I am weak, then I am strong.

2 Corinthians 12:9–10

The LORD is my rock, my fortress and
    my deliverer;
    my God is my rock, in whom I take
      refuge.
He is my shield and the horn of my
      salvation, my stronghold.

Psalm 18:2

SOURCES

Accountability

Philip Yancey, *What's So Amazing About Grace?*
(Grand Rapids: Zondervan, 1997), 275–76

Rodney L. Cooper, *Shoulder to Shoulder*
(Grand Rapids: Zondervan, 1997), 108

Attitude

Oswald Chambers, *My Utmost for His Highest*
(Grand Rapids: Discovery House, 1998),
    January 2 devotion

Charles Stanley, *A Touch of His Love*
(Grand Rapids: Zondervan, 1994), 63

Achievement

Denny Rydberg, *Twentysomething: Life beyond College*
(Grand Rapids: Zondervan, 1991), 149, 151–52

Charles Stanley, *A Touch of His Love*
(Grand Rapids: Zondervan, 1994), 35–36

Change

Denny Rydberg, *Twentysomething: Life beyond College*
(Grand Rapids: Zondervan, 1991), 31

Excerpts from *Bread for the Journey* by
Henri J.M. Nouwen. ©1996 by Henri J.M. Nouwen.
Reprinted by permission of HarperCollins
Publishers, Inc.

Character

John Ortberg, *The Life You've Always Wanted*
(Grand Rapids: Zondervan, 1997), 102–103

Charles Stanley, *A Touch of His Love*
(Grand Rapids: Zondervan, 1994), 91–92

Compassion

Vic Black, *Collegiate Devotional Bible*
(Grand Rapids: Zondervan, 1998), 197

Patrick Kavanaugh, *Spiritual Moments with the
    Great Composers*
(Grand Rapids: Zondervan, 1995), 103–104

Communication

Charles Stanley, *A Touch of His Love*
(Grand Rapids: Zondervan, 1994), 71

Edward G. Dobson, *Simplicity*
(Grand Rapids: Zondervan, 1995), 13

Excerpts from *Bread for the Journey* by
Henri J.M. Nouwen. ©1996 by Henri J.M. Nouwen.
Reprinted by permission of HarperCollins
Publishers, Inc.

Dreams

Jena Borah, *Collegiate Devotional Bible*
(Grand Rapids: Zondervan, 1998), 206

Patrick Kavanaugh, *Spiritual Moments with the
    Great Composers*
(Grand Rapids: Zondervan, 1995), 41–42

Excellence

Patrick Kavanaugh, *Spiritual Moments with the
    Great Composers*
(Grand Rapids: Zondervan, 1995), 51–52

Larry Bauer, *Collegiate Devotional Bible*
(Grand Rapids: Zondervan, 1998), 890

Focus

Charles Stanley, *A Touch of His Love*
(Grand Rapids: Zondervan, 1994), 27–28

Edward G. Dobson, *Simplicity*
(Grand Rapids: Zondervan, 1995), 179–80

Imagination

Christopher de Vinck, *Simple Wonders*
(Grand Rapids: Zondervan, 1995), 115, 24

Rory Noland, *The Heart of the Artist*
(Grand Rapids: Zondervan, 1999), introduction

Leadership

Sid Buzzell, Kenneth Boa, and Bill Perkins, eds.,
The Leadership Bible
(Grand Rapids: Zondervan, 1998), 257

Sid Buzzell, Kenneth Boa, and Bill Perkins, eds.,
The Leadership Bible
(Grand Rapids: Zondervan, 1998), 1258

Priorities

John Ortberg, *The Life You've Always Wanted*
(Grand Rapids: Zondervan, 1997), 20, 24

Ron Blue, *Generous Living*
(Grand Rapids: Zondervan, 1997), 46

Perseverance

Terry Cook, *Collegiate Devotional Bible*
(Grand Rapids: Zondervan, 1998), 193

Tom Yeakley, *Collegiate Devotional Bible*
(Grand Rapids: Zondervan, 1998), 9

Respect

Bill Hybels, *Descending into Greatness*
(Grand Rapids: Zondervan, 1993), 123–25

Carol Rugg, *Collegiate Devotional Bible*
(Grand Rapids: Zondervan, 1998), 1352

Service

Larry Richards, *Wisdom for the Graduate*
(Grand Rapids: Zondervan, 1988), 127–28

John Ortberg, *The Life You've Always Wanted*
(Grand Rapids: Zondervan, 1997), 111

Strength

Mike Edsall, *Collegiate Devotional Bible*
(Grand Rapids: Zondervan, 1998), 157

Bill Hybels, *Descending into Greatness*
(Grand Rapids: Zondervan, 1993), 43

Initiative

Patrick Kavanaugh, *Spiritual Moments with the
Great Composers*
(Grand Rapids: Zondervan, 1995), 38–39

Gary Smalley, *Joy That Lasts*
(Grand Rapids: Zondervan, 1988), 144–45

Innovation

Sid Buzzell, Kenneth Boa, and Bill Perkins, eds.,
The Leadership Bible
(Grand Rapids: Zondervan, 1998), 1168

Sid Buzzell, Kenneth Boa, and Bill Perkins, eds.,
The Leadership Bible
(Grand Rapids: Zondervan, 1998), 1302

Integrity

Steve Rugg, *Collegiate Devotional Bible*
(Grand Rapids: Zondervan, 1998), 46

Kent Walstrom, *Collegiate Devotional Bible*
(Grand Rapids: Zondervan, 1998), 225